W9-BOL-987

SUPERCARS

MARYSA STORM

BLACK
RABBIT
BOOKS

Bolt Jr. is published by Black Rabbit Books
P.O. Box 3263, Mankato, Minnesota, 56002.
www.blackrabbitbooks.com
Copyright © 2020 Black Rabbit Books

Michael Sellner, designer; Omay Ayres, photo researcher

Names: Storm, Marysa, author.
Title: Supercars / by Marysa Storm.
Description: Mankato, Minnesota : Black Rabbit Books,
[2020] | Series: Bolt Jr. Wild rides | Includes bibliographical
references and index. | Audience: Age 6-8. | Audience:
Grade K to 3.
Identifiers: LCCN 2019002771 (print) | LCCN 2019004053
(ebook) | ISBN 9781623101978 (e-book) |
ISBN 9781623101916 (library binding) |
ISBN 9781644661239 (paperback)
Subjects: LCSH: Sports cars–Juvenile literature.
Classification: LCC TL236 (ebook) | LCC TL236 .S765 2020
(print) | DDC 629.222/1–dc23
LC record available at https://lccn.loc.gov/2019002771

Printed in the United States. 5/19

Image Credits
automobiles.honda.com: Honda Motor Company, 7; bugatti.com:
Bugatti Automobiles, 18-19, 21, 22-23; dimmitt.com: Dimmit
Automotive Group, 8-9; ford.com: Ford Media Center, 4; iStock:
mevans, Cover; media.lamborghini.com: Lamborghini Media Center,
16-17; media.lamborghini.com/english: Lamborghini Media Center,
6-7, 12; media.mclarenautomotive.com: McLaren Media, 13, 20-
21; Shutterstock: Creative icon styles, 14; grafixx, 3, 24; John_T,
Cover; Max Earey, 1; slava296, 10; Wasant, 5; ultimatecarpage.
com: Wouter Melissen, 10-11

Contents

CHAPTER 1

A Wild Ride

A **flashy** car roars down the road. It zips through curves. It speeds along **straightaways**. Other cars can't keep up.

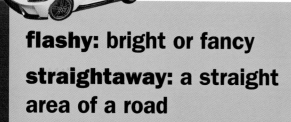

flashy: bright or fancy

straightaway: a straight area of a road

COMPARING
PRICES

2019
Lamborghini
Aventador S
about $420,000

Super Speedy

People drive supercars on streets. But they're built for tracks. They have big engines. They speed up quickly. Supercars are fancy. They're also very expensive.

2019 Honda Accord LX
about $24,000

PARTS OF A
Supercar

wing

wheels

engine

headlights

low body

9

CHAPTER 2

History

People call the Mercedes-Benz 300 SL the first supercar. It came out in 1954. The car was fast. It had **gull-wing doors**. No one had made a car like that before.

gull-wing door: a door that opens upward

Getting Better

In 1966, Lamborghini made the Miura. It had a wide, low body. Companies started making **similar** cars. They became faster and flashier.

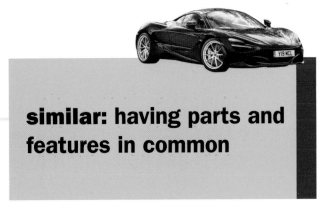

similar: having parts and features in common

Companies That Make Supercars

Great Britain
Aston Martin
Jaguar
McLaren

France
Bugatti

Germany
Audi
Mercedes-Benz
Porsche

Italy
Ferrari
Lamborghini

15

CHAPTER 3

Speeding On

The first supercars amazed drivers. And they've only gotten better. Most go more than 200 miles (322 km) per hour. They have big brakes. They turn quickly.

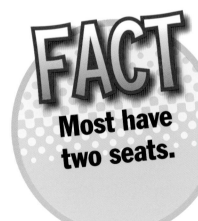

FACT

Most have two seats.

The Future

New supercars will be even better. They'll go even faster. Some could be electric. No matter what, drivers will love them.

◀ · · · · · · · · **Bugatti Chiron's Top Speed**
261 miles
(420 km) per hour

Bonus Facts

The Chiron **costs** about $3 billion dollars.

Supercars have big engines.

Ford only plans to sell 1,350 GTs.

Some people **collect** supercars.

collect: to gather a group of things as a hobby

READ MORE/WEBSITES

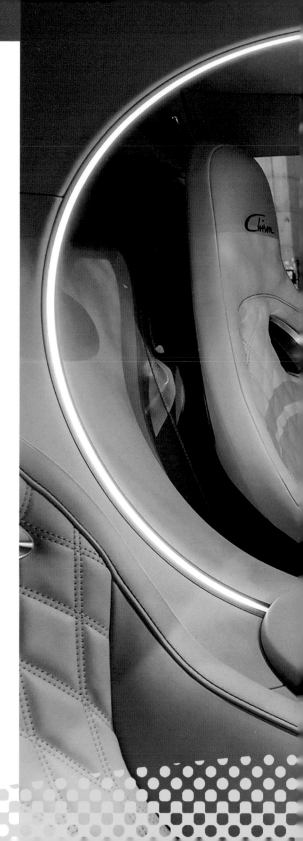

Adamson, Thomas K. *Sports Cars.* Full Throttle. Minneapolis: Bellwether Media, Inc., 2019.

Fishman, Jon M. *Cool Sports Cars.* Awesome Rides. Minneapolis: Lerner Publications, 2019.

Geddis, Norm. *Hop Inside the Most Exotic Cars.* The World of Automobiles. Broomall, PA: Mason Crest, 2019.

Facts about Cars
www.scienceforkidsclub.com/cars.html

Sportscar Facts for Kids
kids.kiddle.co/Sportscar

Sports Cars
www.dkfindout.com/us/transportation/history-cars/sports-cars/

GLOSSARY

collect (KUH-lekt)—to gather a group of things as a hobby

flashy (FLASH-ee)—bright or fancy

gull-wing door (GUHL-wing DOHR)—a door that opens upward

similar (SIM-uh-ler)—having parts and features in common

straightaway (STREYT-uh-wey)—a straight area of a road

INDEX